For Brandon-

My joy, my pride, my light.

In a lively village of Punjab, there lived a girl named Mannat Kaur and her little brother, Bahadur Singh. Their home was always filled with love, laughter, and the yummy smell of their grandmother's cooking.

Mannat and Bahadur were inseperable. They played together in the fields, flew colourful kites, and Mannat danced while Bahadur played the dhol.

Every year, the two siblings eagerly awaited the festival of Rakhri, a day to celebrate their bond. On this day, Mannat would tie a special thread, a rakhri, around Bahadur's wrist. It wasn't just any thread, but a symbol of their love for each other.

In return, Bahadur would give Mannat a present; but the true gift was the love they shared and the promise they made to protect and care for each other.

One year, as Rakhri approached, Mannat was troubled. She wanted to give her brother a rakhri that truly represented their bond, but she didn't know how.

IDEA

She thought and thought, and then she had an idea!
She would weave all of their memories into the rakhri.

Using threads of gold, she wove in their laughter. With threads of blue, she wove in their shared dreams. And with threads of red, she wove in their love and adventures.

When Bahadur saw the rakhri, his eyes filled with tears. “It’s the most beautiful rakhri I’ve ever seen” he said, hugging Mannat.

Bahadur then gave Mannat a small pendant shaped like a heart, representing the heartbeats they shared, and their unbreakable bond.

As the years passed, even when distance separated them, the memories of Rakhri kept them close.

Every year, no matter where they were, they remembered the year of the hand-woven rakhri, and it was a constant reminder of their everlasting bond.

And so, in every corner of the world, as the moon shines bright, siblings come together, celebrating love, life, and the unbreakable bond they share.

Manufactured by Amazon.ca
Bolton, ON